Some Notes You Hold

NEW AND SELECTED POEMS

ALSO BY RITA QUILLEN

NOVELS

Wayland
Hiding Ezra

POETRY

The Mad Farmer's Wife
Her Secret Dream
Counting the Sums
Looking for Native Ground:
Contemporary Appalachian Poetry

We hope you enjoy this Misprint
(crooked cover)

If you feel so inclided, please feel free
to leave a review on Amazon,
Goodreads, our website, or wherever!

Some Notes You Hold

NEW AND SELECTED POEMS

The Madvile Team

RITA SIMS QUILLEN

Donated to the
Shady Shores
Lending Library
10/14/2020

MADVILLE
P U B L I S H I N G

LAKE DALLAS, TEXAS

FIRST EDITION

Requests for permission to reprint or reuse material from this work should be sent to:

Permissions
Madville Publishing
PO Box 358
Lake Dallas, TX 75065

Publication Credits:

Appalachian Anthology-Wiley Cash Edition: "Laughing Ghazal," "The Gospel of Junior," "Why I Hate Honey Locusts"; *Appalachian Heritage*: "My Grandfather Photographs His Son," "Exeunt," "Forest Bathing"; *Appalachian Journal*: "First Christmas" and "First Memory"; *Blue Fifth Review*: "Graveyard Tree," "Grounding," "Tree Gothic," "Why I Love Fall"; *Connotation Online*: "Feeding the Flow," "Taste and Other Mysteries"; *The Dead Mule School of Southern Literature*: "Listening to My Daughter on the Radio" and "Taking Inventory: His Hammer"; *drafthorse: lit journal of work and no work*: "Maybe Tragedy Is Too Strong a Word"; *Girls Like Us: 40 Extraordinary Women Celebrate Girlhood*, edited by Gina Misoroglu, World Library Books, 1999: "Sugar-n-Spice, Etc."; *Her Secret Dream*, Wind Publications, 2007: "My Grandfather Photographs His Son, 1937"; *Potomac Review*: "Texaco Opera"; *Preposterous: Poems of Youth*, edited by Richard Jackson, Orchard, 1991: "Sugar-n-Spice, Etc."; *Prime Number*: "The Gospel of Junior—Garden Rite"; *Something Solid to Anchor To*, Finishing Line Press, 2014: "Something in That Winter Light," "First Memory," "Something Solid to Anchor To," "Maybe Tragedy Is Too Strong a Word," "Witness," "Taking Inventory," "Graveyard Tree," "First Christmas," "Tree Gothic," "Sugar-n-Spice, Etc.," "Waking Up to Life," "Listening to My Daughter on the Radio," "My Grandfather Photographs His Son, 1937"; *Still: The Journal*: "Witness," "Why I Write," "Why I Dance"; *Town Creek Poetry*: "Something Solid to Anchor To"; *The Tusculum Review*: "Fallow Fields"; *Voices*: "Coal Camp Pantoum."

Cover Art: *Layers (Blue Wings)*, 2015, 12" x 12" x 2.5", mixed media on plexiglass and mirror by Suzanne Stryk
Cover Design: Jacqueline Davis
Author Photo: Cyndee Gray Harr

ISBN: 978-1-948692-44-1 Paper, 978-1-948692-45-8 ebook
Library of Congress Control Number: 2020937139

TABLE OF CONTENTS

III. HOLDING ON

Some Notes You Hold

New and Selected Poems

1. LETTING GO

"I recall the bridge as I cross it again.
It seems the hills and rivers have been waiting,
The flowers and willows all are selfless now.
The field is sleek and vivid, thin mist shines,
On soft sand, the sunlight's color shows it's late.
All the traveler's sorrow fades away,
What better place to rest than this?"

—"Traveling Again" by Du Fu, trans. by B. Watson

The Gospel of Junior: A Prologue

The Book of Junior was economical,
only needing a half-dozen commandments:
Gardening is a sacrament,
your tithe paid with hoe and bent back.
Keep everything Godly clean.
Keep the Sabbath, no matter
what the hayfield says.
In fact, go to church every time the door opens
but don't crow about it.
Your life will tell the tale.
Most of all, don't throw things away.
Everything, all of it, is a gift.

My dad's dime-store dungeon of detritus
down in the dark basement was a wonder.
Nothing escaped him,
not the broken or rusty
the warped or the worn.
Dozens of nails driven in joists
held bags of treasure:
screws, nails, nuts and bolts,
belts, brackets, brushes and buckets—
anything you could ever want or need
or never want or need.
His underground hardware was a goldmine
to the tinkerer or child of the Depression.

He could've bought new
but that's heresy
in his anti-prosperity gospel.
Living cheap is living humble.
Transcendence is to be saved
by what's broken,
sanctification sent by self-sufficiency—
Grace from going without.

Junior was the camel
passing through that needle's eye
every day,
a piece of broken pipe in one hand
rusty wire in the other,
his dusty broken-down brogans
with the recycled laces
shuffling down that Redemption Road.

GARDEN RITE

Each spring on his postage stamp of earth the same rituals:
At the first warm breeze out came the two-by-fours
nailed together into a rectangle
where he tenderly pushed lettuce seeds into soft mud
draped the airy muslin covering over it all
like a communion table waiting for the church bell
stepped back and smiled.
Consecrate this crop.

The days had to lengthen
 before the rest could join in.
The old rusty push-plow of his ancestors
a hoe he had kept from the barn of his boyhood—
lifelong tie to the gardens of the dead.
It is right to give thanks and praise.

He used the creek and tree line in April
to sight the straight line that would become
by the hot buzz of August
a choir of corn releasing soft hallelujahs.
Beans would be the kneeling women at the altar,
onions the sour deacons of the doxology,
squash women in yellow bonnets and calico of his youth,
sweet fat cabbage babies wafting and waving,
in the blinding sun's light.
We are what feeds us.

He plunged little crosses in the ground
where tomatoes, smeared with stigmata
of juicy joy, would shine over the garden.
Not a thing wrong with the bread and the wine
but a country boy had to have beans.
No communion wafer unless it was made with ground corn.
Let us keep the feast, lift up our hearts.

And my father, the high priest of the scriptural lines
of this bright dusty kingdom,
giving absolution with green garden hose in days of drought
would know precisely when to slowly lift the cloth
from that communion table, pinch tender shoots
to lay on his tongue, just the tiniest bite.

Take and eat.
This refuge, this is all—

Our salad days.

GROUNDING

When Dad stepped out the back door
he met Clinch Mountain's majestic face,
her specter changing from green to gold
to gray and black and back again—
reference point eternal
as year after year clicked faster by.

To his right, he could see
through trees' bare winter arms
the home he was born in,
the pasture where he ran and cried
when first his father, then his grandfather died,
leaving him alone in a house of women.
He could see his cattle
grazing up there now, unaware
of any tragedy, peacefully breathing
under the mountain's shadow and wind.

To his left, the church
that centered his days, built on land
deeded by great-grandfather,
cornerstone dragged
from that same mountain mother.
Its organ and piano rang,
rang through his days
just like the big bell
on its steeple overhead
his family had also helped hang up there
had prayed under, mourned under,
that often brought a smile to his face
with its noon tune as he plowed,
planted, pulled and hauled in his garden
merely yards away,
smiling at this life in the shadows
of all he was or could be

living where everything had happened that mattered—
everything that mattered had happened—
he could see it all right there
on that one little spot so small
invisible even to the heavens.

But to say it was a small life
is to misunderstand.
What profiteth a man to rush about,
live big, move off to hostile climates,
losing sight of that long arc
of loss and longing and love.
It is a special gift to bloom
where you're planted,
grown in the fine sand
of blind luck and whimsy,
the tiny cosmos of root, stem, and vein.

EXEUNT

So now it's winter again yet
sunrise and sunset make us forget
so stunning the color spraying from ridges.
In the icy clear brittle blue air above,
the mountain grays like a grandmother,
death strolls close by—the mundane maudlin.
It would be fitting to go then.

But you left in summer
when sweet calves quivered on new legs,
peepers and lightning bugs surfaced at gloaming
supplying the soundtrack of summer.
The hayfield was high green grace,
leaves reaching their full glory
bluebirds nesting, soft stems of new irises
waving in the wind's parade.

Why then?
Why not wait until it would be easier to let go?
I think it was to carry the color with you
in the soul's eye,
go out on top
in the highest of high notes
wearing the beauty shroud
to remind us all our last day
will be sudden and bright.

Witness

My father owned silence
the way seasons own the trees.
He avoided words,
used looks, gestures, altered breathing
but nothing dramatic usually.
Emotion is what occurred
at other people's houses.

I guess that's why this clings like beggar lice:
After one of many long days when he missed supper
working two jobs he finally sat down at 9
before a plate that was four hours old.
I froze in disbelief in the doorway
when he threw a slice of mushy tomato
from his plate at my mother
standing at the sink,
missed her and hit the just-ironed curtain.
Her stiff back a signboard of rage and hurt,
she didn't even turn around,
the only sound the splashing of the dishwater
that hid her hands while he ate and
I backed away, backed away from them
silent witness to their silent witness
the soft heart of the tomato
a blood red flag
by my mother's head.

First Christmas

I wish I was
I want to be 1
who can quote chapter and verse
& just go on & don we now our gay apparel
build a fire roasting chestnuts
me of the 30-year Santa collection
3 Christmas trees every hall
decked out, goofy sweaters, presents
for everyone bells and snowmen
& tinsel and wreaths stale as Claxton fruitcake joy to the world
1 of the wise men is missing and the star, too
fa la la la lifetime of Kodak moments he was never in
but behind the lens except that 1 in the cheap Santa suit
cotton-ball beard he wore every year
my baby sister's eyes and mouth a perfect
O holy night of fear and awe not recognizing the stick-skinny
Santa with grease under his nails let nothing you dismay let
nothing you dismay.

Maybe Tragedy Is Too Strong a Word

I hadn't slept but a couple of hours.
  Excitement charged the air. At daylight all six of us piled in that Ford Fairlane
  —our perpetual clown car. Twenty dollars a payday stuffed in his sock drawer
  fueled my father's plan; long days, longer nights in the factory were now
  funding the redemption close at hand. Once we hit South Carolina the road
  flattened out, the sky doubled. Gulls flew honor escort.

Factory workers with 4 kids can't afford beachfront.
  But a street back we could smell the sea. My sisters spilled their suitcases
  Mother had spent hours packing and in minutes our father was leading
  the parade snaking across the street and down the dune all white bellies and legs
  marching into the sea. We hit the waves, surf so rough we could barely
  stand. I saw the black cloud way out on the horizon, the dark look crowding
  my father's features. After less than an hour, the pouring rain drove us in.
  It rained and rained and rained. We didn't even want to go scour the junk shops
  for those outhouse salt and pepper shakers, and turtles, and porpoises
  all with Myrtle Beach, SC on the side.

Six crammed into a small hotel room watching soap operas, the two little ones
  bickering. It stopped raining on the third day, our last day, and we scurried
  back out into the salty froth. The sea was almost solid white, still breaking
  from the constant wind. The little ones could only splash at the edge. One
  big wave knocked me down, picked me up, sent me tumbling end over end,
  life blurred, I drowned for a minute, then the wave's hard hand hammered
  my head straight into the sand, filled my ears, nose, lungs with the
  stinging brine. I crawled out with matted hair, spit out of the sea
  a beached mermaid. "Let's go." My father seemed a few inches shorter.
  The sadness sat on all of us, an anchor weight on our chests.

He didn't speak all the way home unless he had to. I got to ride up front with him.
  By dark, down to the last long curvy road toward home, the sudden fatigue
  of a year's savings wasted, another year looming standing over that hot machine
  in a room with no air, a life without a breeze, had reached his cellular level.
  He aged 10 years. He started taking the curves on the wrong side of the road
  as home and factory and life got closer and closer. Is he trying, I wondered,
  to kill us all? Maybe he thinks that's best. "It will take me a week,"
  my mother said over my left shoulder. "There's sand everywhere. Everything
  is gritty."
Indeed.

Taking Inventory: His Hammer

You always appreciated good tools.
Your Craftsman hammer fits balanced
perfect in the hand.
I grip the worn faded pink center
of the red handle
turn the smooth silver face to mine
see the pale reflection
blur to abstraction,
then drive the white nail home
with one blow.

Laughing Ghazal

Somewhere on the ribbon's DNA is the laugh.
The call of our mountain tribe's joy and bond—the laugh.

Cackle of guinea, wail of hound, turkey putt chorus
a whole army of happy hyenas, all who laugh.

Wind creaks screen door's squeaking hinge, eyes closed, embracing it.
My dad and his trio of sisters live for the laughs.

Grandson goes limp with joy at my clowning, freeing it,
hears a loud bird sail above, calling love out with laughs.

Somewhere in my Book of Life I am gifted that laugh
marked forever with joy's gene, and with them all I laugh.

Apple Butter

The spring burst of white blossoms
keeps its promise.
My mother's tree is a good one.

October's cool blue sky
lures out the wooden paddle and kindling,
the black kettle nesting in the basement,
a congregation of clean jars
ready for the yearly rite.

While the fire licks the kettle clean
burning the cinnamon smell into our clothes,
my mother's hands
smooth the last quarter-moon apple
out of the pan.
I remember the mounds of peels
wormholes and rotten places.
My mother's knife cuts true.

We wait silently side by side
stirring.
When the bubbles and steam are thick,
she signals it's ready.
The jars are lined up
wide-mouthed
to receive the blessing.
This year I am old enough
to fill them up.

We pour.
In the thick smell
spring comes to fall.

We carry the jars to the basement
where they wait to be called up,

a reserve of past plenty,
denying the power of winter
down in the dark cool heart
of the house.

PRAYER FOR LEAVING

Let us hold the hand of memory one moment more.
Keep the stopped clock of change from ticking.
Walking back into my daughter's bedroom
after dropping her off at college, I heard it—
the same sob that would sound at my father's grave,
at my last glance back before I put the key in the door
for the final time where my babies and I were once young.

Leaving is grieving, one and the same.
What was now isn't, space and time
full or empty in a new way.
Every new place I move is quieter,
everything continuously going somewhere else
except me and the silence.

May my hand clasp its mate as they rest together under my chin
propping up a prayer and a bowed head before lifting,
helping me rise to the day and the dawn and the darkness.
Let them work together kneading the bread to full measure,
playing a tune, soothing restless spirits.
Help the past stay where it is and my wary feet move on.

Letter to My Grandfather

Grandpa, he has really missed you.
The house you left needed repairs
porch floor caved in
fence posts fell out like rotted teeth,
the stone wall would not stand.
Somehow, he knew how to fix all those things
even growing up in a house of women.
Work became his only companion.
He took to solitude like a monk.
The barn was his convent,
the cows black-robed sisters
who pray special prayers for the solitary.
He mows down weeds and saplings,
keeps your ground with precision.
Everybody needs a mission—
his was to figure out
how to be a man without you around
how to grow the perfect garden
how to tend this ground.

Graveyard Tree

I groaned when I saw it
knowing its coming intrusion
on my thoughts, dreams, words, again and again.
A crow streaks overhead—the maudlin is calling!
His grave is barely out from under its shade
and just his body length from the road
always just missing the good
perched on the edge of bad.
The marker is exquisite
a bucolic scene carved in the bronze,
an icon of a whole life
in bas-relief I trace with a finger
trying to read the Braille of almost 78 years
rewriting some of it as I go.

My grandmother, grandfather, an aunt, friends,
all spread across different gardens of the cemetery
north, south, east, west
and grand statuary—white marble scarecrows
warning off the living.
It's not peaceful here, what with the blood rush
and birds and disassociative screaming
going on in my head.
I won't be joining them here ever.
We have plots near his family—
you know, all that Biblical cleaving and such
so I try to spend some time now
looking for Art, Beauty, Truth
The Grand Deception offered
in this absolute empty desolate
quiet.

My Grandfather Photographs His Son

The man behind the camera
smiles as the developing image
floats up from the water
he carefully swirls
in his wellhouse darkroom,
the face of his only son—
his name carrier—
resting in his eyes:

My father's face a rising sun
in a world of sepia shadow and gray
posed before a punched tin pie safe
his chin tilting up cocky, comfortable.
Tattered overalls and broken-down shoes
contrast with the snazzy fedora and wire glasses.
He is a little man rising up
leaning forward, fingers gripping
the red rocker's arms
getting on with life,
set loose on the world:

Not long after, this world crashed down,
my grandfather died—
the happy little man in the picture, too,
replaced by a somber old soul.
I cradle the pictures in my hand
feel the light particles move—
all three of us one
trinity of regret.

Taste and Other Mysteries

Dad poured packs of peanuts
in those small Coke bottles
washing all that good salt
into a sugary brine
and bland mush,
loved chicken livers fried crisp
(even the smell makes me gag),
delighted in candied orange slices
with the consistency of sugared plastic for dessert.

He would pour out a whole jar of canned tomatoes
—edible dreamcatchers floating in red soup—
and relish them with peanut butter crackers.

Junior was the only person
in the entire world
who actually loved Claxton fruitcake.

Worst of all, most repulsive snack ever—
those little flat cans with a key on top
which he would roll back
to reveal a smelly treasure:
little oily sardines to lay on saltines
which he would make disappear
into the smile under his moustache.

How does one reconcile it?
Sound judgment otherwise,
his brain was hardwired to change flavors
from reality to some phantom or dream,
into delicacies inexplicable to me,
eating memories, perhaps,
from another age, another place,
where he was a fatherless child,
his mother too sad to get out of bed.

All I know is he would laugh out loud
at this remembering
while hating all the attention—
no opportunity to defend himself
or explain or qualify.

As someone famously said,
no one wants a poet in the family.
He's not here to forgive me
place the calloused hand of absolution
on my shoulder giving me permission
to go work another field, plant some other seed
try a new recipe.

But it's time.
I am old now, too,
with my own strange cravings.
I have worked his garden
captured his countenance
kept a legend of all his accounts
made a record of his days
served up his plate
hued the jagged field rock of his life
into a smooth stone necklace
I wear near my heart
as I set my own table
prepare a new feast.

SOMETHING IN THAT WINTER LIGHT

I thought of you today
when brown leaves rained from racing clouds
and the sky burned through, fierce blue.
Rushing air hummed and droned
like an organ bass pedal.
Trees jerked and bowed in amber light.
I placed you among them
a paper doll on a bright page
just beyond the fence
letting you lean
on your shovel or rake or hoe
look long and longer
at what you're missing.

I thought of you today
your back to me, head down
walking away to some other place
where light is all golden.
Just as in life,
you are somewhere else
a slow-moving figure in the garden
parting a mountain meadow far off
fixing, mending, digging
salvaging whatever you can.
You never speak in these visions.
You would think I wouldn't bother
to dream without gifting us
all those missing words.
The wind rushes along, one sound
and syllable, whispering "See."

I thought of you today
when brown leaves rained from racing clouds.

SKELETON TRUTH

I have my mother's hands
that ache in cold and fatigue.
I grimace at any pressure.

More obtuse than hers
lacking grace, clumsy as a boy's,
they dart aimlessly as I speak.

No delicate touch
except at the keyboard
no fingerprints
from years of guitar.

Skin paper thin
blue veins mapping
I search for creams,
a potion to erase the dry curse:
gift of my father's gene pool.

Wrinkling visibly hour to hour
reflecting time's mirror
I have my mother's bones only
my father's skin and moods.

First Memory

People never believe me
when I tell them I recall
waking in my crib, lying watchful
while my parents dozed.
I slept there until I was two
in front of the window in their bedroom.
I remember watching the sun rise
amazed, lazy in my warm nest,
only the sound of breathing,
blood rush pulsing the words *yes* and *yes*.
Just as now I feel no need
to summon others at the moment
the miraculous occurs,
I couldn't tell my parents then or later
that I saw God and angels and clouds
that became beliefs, most of all,
that silence was now
a cloak I would inhabit,
walk around inside
wearing it as beautiful silk
all my days.

II. INTERLUDE: SELAH

"I will incline my ear to a proverb; I will solve my riddle to the music of the lyre."

—Psalm 49 (ESV)

Some Notes You Hold

(There were Native American tribes who built platforms in their cornfields where the women kept watch near harvest time, singing continuously to frighten away animals.)

On a barnwood stage built by their men
above a green ballet of corn and blue curtain of sky,
the women take turns, daylight to daylight
singing and clapping, beating drums
that take their men to war.
Deer and turkey stalk the rows
unless this symphony in the silks
lifts through the tree canopy like thin smoke.
Theirs is a holy chorus:
wolf howl, cooing doves, hallelujah magpies
cawing crows answered in a minor key
chanting ancient sorrows to God and wind.

A small girl walks with her mother
for the very first time to the field
to learn what singing is.
This here is a note, her mother says,
and sounds out a perfect sweet C
with vibrato swift as hummingbird wings.
All you need to know of singing, she says,
whether in church or corn:
Some notes you hold, some you let go.

I have never sung to corn
but have put everything else aside
to let my voice clear the air
slicing clean as the bone-handled knife
that freed the cob from the stalk.
Melody has broken bread and beans
delivered blood red baby tomatoes
to wide-mouthed chalices,
washed mud from squash and onions

29

soothed tender lettuce in its cool bath
pieced a day back together to a 4-beat line,
hummed the doxology of earthly delights—
all the savory songs of soil and seed.
Some notes you hold, some you let go.

WHY I DANCE

It's the lifting, defying the heron's physiology
the whoosh of the heft of all that weight
leaving gravity behind on the creek's glass face
that I feel, lifted by the fiddler's hand,
weightless for that split second
when both left and right foot are off the floor.
I lift my arms out like the climbing hawk
soaring over the still world beneath
moving through pockets of hot and cool air
floating like a note on the evening's breath.
My hard heel beats like the woodpecker's beak
on the old tree bones beneath me
drumming out the tune's heartbeat
in a smiling choir of souls in motion.
The fiddler and I lock eyes and smile
wordless, weightless all at once
joyfully alive in buoyant youth
my feet and his hands together,
warbler and chickadee rising to the dusk
until the song ends,
only the nightingale's song ringing long and strong.

WAKING UP TO LIFE

In memory of Janette Carter

How does the mind of a child know
which moments to cling to,
to remember because
they are doors you step through
never to return to the old rooms?
What signaled the synapses and pathways
to hold this shard of memory, I wonder:

I open my eyes in darkness and shadow
not recognized, hearing soft notes faint and sweet.
I think, *this is it—it's the call.*
Graves are yawning, my Sunday School teacher
flying up like a chimney bat,
neighborhood saints gone from their beds.
A little more awake, I know
it's not a trumpet I hear
but an autoharp
playing a song I recognize,
a Carter Family song,
flowing first like a waterfall,
like a beautiful woman's laugh
then carrying all possible sadness and solace
in the same deep note.

Then I remember where I am—
not at home in bed with my little sister
but in my best friend's bedroom—
at Janette Carter's home
where this fellow insomniac keeps trying
to put things right every night
playing and singing her life
into a song with at least one little good thing—
a happy chorus.

Why I Sing

Here on the farm
you are surrounded by music.
The tree frogs rival the Sunday morning church.
Whippoorwills have finally returned to silky evening air.
Coyotes howl their threats
in perfect pentatonic harmony!
Gobblers operatic answers bounce
from ridge to rock,
black crows bark and shriek,
katydids sing the doxology
as we head inside for sleep.
Why we are gifted this is a mystery.
So, who am I to stand mute and dead?
Singing is lifting, light as flour, to the quiet.
When you sing, no one can tell the difference
whether you're laughing, crying, raging, grieving,
loving, lusting, or running for your life.
I close my eyes and pull in the silent note
then free it.
It always packs up pain
for the road and off they go
out onto the great flow
the rest of the mad choir's offering.

Fiddler's Suite

For fiddlers Charlie Mack Daugherty, Joe Goode, Uncle Charlie Osborne, and Beachard Smith

The chinrest familiar as your sweet babies' heads
cradled with the same smile,
frog of the bow held
like your sweetheart's sweet hand.
You knew the fretboard like your own mind
played mostly without sight, eyes closed
or blinded by a stray bullet.

Music was the creek you swam in
lifting you light as leaf litter to float.
You were the song of the sharecropper's son
sipped from the little brown jug you saved
horsehair filaments flying about your face.

A fiddle is fretless, no signposts along your way.
Your fingers must be taught home
to the exact spot where music lives,
a centimeter either way bringing
nothing more than noise.
Playing requires backbone of cedar,
heart wide as the river,
spirit open and at risk every moment
yet strong enough to stand
all the sadness and sweet longing
sparked by your fingertips
releasing tones and tunes
of forever's long memory
with just a touch.

Why I Play Music

It is a kind of death
without consequences—
the death of words
sweet, sweet silence
only the soundless hum of electrical impulse
putting my finger
grooved and scarred as the poplar's bark
on precisely the right string on that sweet neck—
a millimeter for a millisecond
bringing the note we need.
How is it possible to be so alive and busy,
without consciousness, without language?
Oh, to be shed of syllables and their weight,
to just know without knowing
and naming how you know,
just like I knew the sound of my daughter's cry
amongst the din of the hospital nursery,
truly a consummation devoutly to be wished,
like the hognose snake roiling
her mortal coil on the ground in front of me
to scare me away from her babies.
She functions fine without language
her life one long song unceasing,
her life just a series of notes,
a throat-singing victory every day.

Listening to My Daughter on the Radio

Her heart when I first heard it—
a snare drum brush sound
through the stethoscope.
A few months later
a piercing cry
sharp as a paper cut
that I recognized—
recognized from way down the hall—
stunned by nature's imprinting,
how my sex altered my senses.
I knew her cry.

Far away from me now
in every way
the strong voice on the radio
plays what she wants
says so, says so
cracks wise to her river buddies
quotes herself, nicknames herself
floating along on a current
of ions charged
positive and negative and immutable
a life in 4/4 time.

WHY I WALK

It is another way to make music,
my heels clicking out rhythm
dancing across the pasture road,
my breath the tune
breaking between pulse beats
of yet unwritten lines,
rising and falling in waves
like the mountain ridgeline above.

I take in the scene
but mostly keep a keen eye
on the staff running under my feet.
The inertia running sole to crown
builds to crescendo of image and sound.
Looking down brings
magic words that become song—
bass and treble clef
flushing up suddenly as a grouse
or a startled buck.

Under gargoyle clouds in a mountain cathedral
the shuffling of my feet becomes a fiddle bow
on the catgut-strung meadow they travel.
I wait patiently to hear
the whole symphony of thoughts—
ballad or fugue
rondo or reel.

Pressing on into headwind toward the light
moving into that silence after music ends,
I pull my jacket tighter over my heart
quicken my step
relishing the melody of measure
after measure after measure
of memory.

Texaco Opera

At Grandpa's Texaco Station, I loved Saturday night's sound:
the ding of gas pump bell and a pure soprano voice
blurred memory of kerosene smell and pipe smoke.
Notes whispering from his big radio like chills or snippet of dream
my face like Grandpa's, in faraway reverie, lips lifting,
smiling at new rooms opening in our head, rising from the notes.

It was the women who drew me, heart tethered to their notes,
male voices leaving me unmoved, impatient with their dark sound
discovering then the escape offered by treble lines lifting,
eyes closed, high above black lace sky, shyly testing my voice.
The Metropolitan Opera was unreal as wealth, a dream
where women in lavish dresses made music visible as smoke.

Grandpa was a long way from coal-camp smoke—
even further from polished pages of his calligraphy left in love notes,
long way from gorgeous European cities of his soldier daydreams—
coal trucks on 23. Clinchfield train whistle blasting background sound—
shrill earsplitting noise, nothing like magic Renée Fleming's unearthly voice
drowning it all out every Saturday night by fireside with pipe smoke lifting.

Maria Callas and Joan Sutherland, even their names brought a lifting.
Carmen, Figaro, Madama Butterfly, Don Giovanni fill my head like smoke.
They sang in foreign tongue, yet I still recognized the voice.
Writing letters only to burn them in *La Bohème*, Tosca dies while writing notes.
Even so young, I see in words and tunes the power of sound,
the way hand, lips, tongue and heart could create a daylight dream.

To return here to his boyhood home had been Grandpa's fevered dream
only his father's death made possible long night's lifting.
Like Tosca he found hope for a future in the turning key sound
of his father's farmhouse door, a remembered fireplace spreading hope in the smoke.
Heart overflowing, writing all his soldier friends excited notes,
he told how he'd escaped the drudgery of coal, found a businessman's voice.

Sitting by the stove, I remember the woman at church with her noon bell voice.
To sing of poets, geisha girls, soldiers and fair maids, a wondrous dream.
It would take a lot of growing to hold those notes,
my own little prayed secret, one nobody would be lifting.

In coal camp, nothing's pretty and chimneys spew black gritty smoke.
I needed to be near music, not trains or coal trucks' sound.

A little blond girl huddles beside a kerosene stove, notes lifting
the voice in her head straight to heaven with Grandpa's pipe smoke
treble trill and stunning vibrato fueling dreams of living inside that sound.

III. HOLDING ON

"Human life—a dream of joy and sorrow mingled;
Why is it that, gaining one, the other also comes?"

—"An Allegory" by Yu Xuanji, trans. by Leonard Ng

Deep Dark Suite

I.

Dark is not always deep.
Deep is not always dark.

Seven people living in a school bus
up the cool hollow from our tidy brick
in my dreamlike childhood.
Dark but not deep.

The perfect math of the spider web
woven in pasture gate by a nightmare
with a potbelly and six legs.
Deep but not dark.

The flood that came a solid wall
of water off High Knob,
washing away house and man,
seen smoking his last cigarette,
red light fire of the end
blinking as water took it all.
Dark but not deep.

II.

The hognose snake rolled out in our path,
stood tall and puffed its hood, weaving its spell,
meaning to scare us out of our shoes.
When we didn't move,
she roiled and writhed, coiling and coiling
like a scarf in a storm,
then stretched motionless, playing dead.
We were transfixed. This is a hoax—
a wondrous hoax—
meant to lure us from her babies

somewhere close by but blind
to her bravery, to her willingness
to sacrifice everything but them.

How deep, this mothering, and dark, too,
all of us blind children.

III.

Almost all the young ones are marked.
Blind to their own beauty
they burn black, red, purple scars
of foreign tongues and ancient symbols
into their arms and back.
Dark, the burns, but not deep
though they like to think so
hoping the naming and etching
into skin will dent the yin,
will count as truth
leave a lasting mark,
but leaving a mark is still leaving,
which is deep but not dark.

IV.

I walk my favorite lane
out the pasture gate
through grapevines and green canopy.
"The woods are lovely, dark and deep,"
I hear the poet say,
as if the three are connected,
ingredients baked into the cake we eat
here in our own Eden
with the Fruit of Knowledge—
the forbidden compote.
So this is my theory of everything:
Life and what comes after
is lovely, dark and deep.

The water washes away.
The vines tangle like family.
The ink spreads across the shoulder
and the mark is left.
We are not there to see it.

After all the trouble, all the years,
it comes down to this.
Dark is not always deep.
Deep is not always dark.

PRAYER FOR BIRDS AND SUNRISE

Thank you for the porch facing east
where I watch each morning
God's hot palm rise
above the mountain's soft sides
fingers spread wide
against a gray pink canvas,
tender light building a silkscreen
to catch drops of worry, sorrow or regret
blown across my hot cup's surface.

May I hear forever the birds above
ones, twos, and triplets of feathered music
floating and darting the currents,
their notes an art song of holy noise
from ancient studios of creation
before love was a word, or grief,
before time became a ghost
breaking glass in the rooms upstairs.

Let the fingered dawn launch the raptor
to carry my heart to deepest secrets of trees,
my feet to the wild creek, my hands together
and head up, walking straight and strong
to fox den, bee tree, deer bed—
places where I wait for the truest rejoicing.

WHY I LOVE FALL

In January's gray mist,
the wind howls, ice crunches.
March brings raucous birds and bugs.
In summer it's man alive and machine, too,
buzzing and banging all over everything.

Fall is the quiet time.
Every day you wake up
waiting for something.
The September hush arrives
with only the slightest rustle,
air hanging full of words
like tree branches lined with wrens.
Then poems start to stop by
lighting here for a rest
as they migrate
to wherever they hibernate.

Since I was a child, I knew
autumn's gift was not just color,
coolness and the high blue canopy,
but knowledge of time passing,
quiet that hurts,
a slant of light
that falls over the face like a veil
hot current of words
coursing overhead
my limbs shedding leaves
that carry poems.

What good has this wisdom brought me?
I will die in more pain than most.

Yet still I keep reaching,
calling out to syllables in sunlight.
I lift an arm and whistle:
Come to me,
here in the color and quiet.

Upon Visiting the Buffalo Bill Museum in Cody, Wyoming

Staring long at the painting
Paiute ghost dancers
frozen forever in mid-step
around a campfire
under the total eclipse of 1889
believing the dance
would lead to removal
of demon whites,
I chuckle at the universe's burnt offering—
the event and the words—
the ghost dance
pure godsend to a poet
who can connive and contrive
art and artifice
from far smaller, baser matters,
speak to national angst
draw approving groans and sighs
from the local college poetry club
just razzle and dazzle
arabesque all the way
to some big prize.

A new eclipse
is coming in August,
so they say.
I think about back home in the mountains.
Here, ghosts are no abstraction.
The hauntings are haunting,
pervasive and inescapable.
So many graceless grannies
hover over supper tables
hollow-eyed gray grandpas
creak the rocker after dark.
Crushed miners and stillborns pose

under the same shade tree
along the childhood creek.
We don't need the eclipse
to see them.

Black or bright,
they're on every corner
not trying to run anybody off
or win a prize
or have high hopes
or change history
or become a poem.

Why I Hate Honey Locusts

Most miss the difference between city and country,
thinking concrete vs. mud, gray vs. green,
but clearly it is the city's muffled metaphors
that separate the two the most,
asphalt and false light
shielding contact with the eternal.

The farm is a hothouse of signs and portents—
all that birthing and dying back,
the roulette weather wheel spinning,
spinning sky, bird, beast, wind,
all harmonizing to shout Solomon's echo:

Here, I am the Rose of Sharon,
the Lily of the Valley.
You won't meet God
at the corner of 34th and Vine,
won't eat of the Tree of Good and Evil
at some hotdog stand.

Here, it is continuous simulacra:
      The snake is Satan.
      The dove is peace.
      The coyote is greed.
      The honey locust a reminder of the sacrifice of Christ.

In Cherokee legend, the locust's long thorns
were the universal test:
If you pierced your skin with one
as you made your way
to work or hunt or lover
and escaped the nightmarish, oozing sore,
then you were touched
by the Great One,
your sentence commuted by Grace.

Today modern Medicine Men have created
a honey locust without any thorns
for city dwellers
who can't handle all that symbolism,
content to be mortals and be done with it,
while out here on the farm
God cracks heads with dropping walnuts,
startles with shrieking hawk,
transfigures the night sky
with a thousand streaks of silent lightning
miles and miles away,
striking all at once,
and the honey locust thorns
scar us deep with those hellish spikes,
wound everyone I know
who has encountered them—
as has love.

TREE GOTHIC

I. Blood Tree

I loved the tree for its shade
the dark gift it offered
and for the gory memory:
My neighbor's grandson Johnny
hidden in the high limbs,
the neighborhood wild child
hurls an ax up into the rustling leaves.
I thought of Fess Parker.
Johnny didn't scream, only grunted
climbed slowly carefully
down one side of his body
a solid red plate of blood
while his sister wailed like some sick bird
Will he die? Will he die?
I thought of Poe
while wild child walked away
head down, not running
not looking back
epitaph written.

II. Trees with Ropes

What is it about swinging from trees?
Some ancient mitochondrial need
to bond with birds—
an arrogant attempt to break the law
of gravity—
the hunger of prepubescent girls
for some touch—
the air moving the hair on our unshaved legs—
for whatever reason
our trees
always had ropes in them.

Coal Camp Pantoum

Straight is the gate and narrow the way
between the shotgun shacks filled with lamplight
so close you could hear your neighbors sigh
smell everybody's beans with fatback and cornbread.

Between the shotgun shacks filled with lamplight
my mother drew figures in the dirt, dreamed of cities
smelled everybody's beans with fatback and cornbread
pretended she was Shirley Temple on the Good Ship Lollipop.

My mother drew figures in the dirt, dreamed of cities,
paying no attention to the oily slag heap at the edge of town,
pretended she was Shirley Temple on the Good Ship Lollipop
cozy in the dark movie theatre every Saturday afternoon.

Paying no attention to the oily slag heap at the edge of town
her brothers chose to follow Gene Autry out to the Painted Desert.
Cozy in the dark movie theatre every Saturday afternoon,
they shrugged when one of the company houses emptied out.

Her brothers chose to follow Gene Autry out to the Painted Desert.
They climbed the slag piles but stayed away from the mine's opening.
They shrugged when one of the company houses emptied out
looked away from the eyes of fatherless boys the mine created.

They climbed the slag piles but stayed away from the mine's opening
that broad dark hole that could lead to destruction,
looked away from the eyes of fatherless boys the mine created.
Straight is the gate and narrow the way.

Sugar-n-Spice, Etc.

All us girls knew about sin
sought after it.
Torn pieces of brown paper bags
wrapped around dried corn silks
secretly cured in the toolshed
supplied cigarettes to wave around
like those women on the soap operas.
In my friend's playhouse
we practiced kissing
furtive and ashamed.
A high-powered telescope
Santa Claus brought
opened up the mysteries
of neighborhood bedrooms.

Once we sneaked out of a slumber party
tiptoed onto an icy bridge
still in our babydoll pajamas and
froze our prissy asses off
to watch the sun stick out its tongue
at the gray world.
Then there was that Halloween
we rolled a septic tank
into the middle of the highway
and set it afire.
It took about 20 state troopers
two tow trucks and a tractor
to move that white-hot donut.
We were fairly disappointed
when nobody got arrested.
Our reputations weren't the best,
but at least what we were made of
wouldn't melt in your mouth.

Something Solid to Anchor To

I.

That's what they sent him after
the old man and his mule
high into Clinch Mountain:
to bring the cornerstone of the new church.
But it was the mule
who turned to stone
halfway up the rocky face
refused to budge.
The old man had never seen him
freeze this solid before.
No sound stirred except the gnats
his breath and the bridle creaking
in the heat while they both waited,
hot currents blurring the view of the high meadow.

II.

She stood before the cracked mirror
twisting and twisting long curls around her fingers
her dead babies' faces scattered out
to her peripheral vision like exploding stars.
She pressed her face to the screen door
looked toward the mountain
as if she would see him up there
so far away, so far away
as he always was.

III.

So he left and walked on alone
Dusty the mule still frozen in place
until he made it to the stream,
light-headed and dizzy from heat
and the bad heart he didn't know he had.

Sitting on a flat rock so smooth and cool
it felt like the chair bottoms he planed.
He watched a trout yawp at a surface bug
while minnows scattered in perfect unison
and Dusty appeared suddenly behind him.

IV.

She thought about the satchel in the closet
packed as always, money sewn into the lining.
She imagined the smell of the burning coal
and the click of the rails as she rolled off
to her new life but she didn't want
her cornbread to burn
so she went back to the stove
pulled out the steaming, sweet loaf
and raised up in time to see a glint of light
out the window beyond the crib and cattle
from the mountainside where she knew
he must be.

V.

Now the sweat was squirting
but he had it, he had the bedrock
pulled from the creek somehow by divine intervention—
God rules the mules, too.
Dusty was lathered now, his breathing labored.
so they stopped and swayed a while
and he saw her in the doorway,
knew about the satchel and the coat
and that he could find her
no matter what train she got on.
She would come back when he asked
just like before.
She just wanted to be sought after and found.
He liked miraculous retrievals,
finding something solid to anchor to.

The Mad Farmer's Wife Learns of Forest Bathing

I would have loved a creek bath but didn't dare,
only chuckled at the saucy thought.
That wasn't what the term meant anyway.
In Japan it's called *shinrin yoku*
my daughter said, forest bathing,
where you go to the woods to renew
to soothe, to relax, to change on the inside.

Country people had always just called it walking.

Striking out across uneven ground
the fat trees welcome us, whispering
a breathless hello.
Our feet drink from the heavy dew
wash the soul clean,
breezes erasing the world
and its cash out of our eyes.
Branches clap their approval—take a bow.

We all pulse along, a kind of wind ourselves,
stop under a red maple veil
in a wedding tent of sleepy poplars,
xylem and cambium rooting us
to a wildness of spirit
as the rooted ones wave us on.

Why I Take Photos

In the beginning was the Word and other words
but even the poet knows, like the prophet
sometimes no syllable can replace the light
the clarity of a framed edge
where truth begins and ends
without that extra step of translation.
The camera's mechanical eye—
its false iris—never lies,
brings color and shadow right past the mind,
past all that annoying logic
straight to the heart of the matter,
which is really to say the gut
where we eat that beauty and joy up.

Love Poem to Trees

If we surrendered
to earth's intelligence
we could rise up rooted, like trees.
—Rainer Maria Rilke

To think, most know nothing of them,
rarely encountering them,
unlucky in their geography
of sand, bushes, or driftwood
or only a few kinds of our tall guardians.

I live in the World's Fair of Trees—the Appalachians—
with every kind, size, color,
every flavor of bark and texture.
Our history is our geography, the writer said.
What Book of Life would have been written
if I had walked only on sand,
on a flat glass plane of grass,
walked in mostly sky,
not enclosed by a family of woods
the arms of the mountains?
How different it must be
to age to the beat of the surf
or the wind howl of the plains.

The old ones knew of tree medicine
the salves and cough tonic
given by sassafras and tulip poplar
the antiseptic pine, the healing hickory—
balm for burns and creaking bones.
They knew, too, the shade and protection,
cut or standing,
how they could stand and cool
or fall and warm them—
daily sacrifices of their tall quiet friends.

Beneath is the understory
which survives
despite the hovering, smothering top.

No one knows their names
except for some so notorious
they are cursed
with the label "Poison."

At roll call each morning
they report:
Mayapple—bug umbrellas
Fern—the ground's cooling fan
Periwinkle—blue sparks on green carpet
Laurel—home for all fur and feathers.

Surrounded by millions of dead skeletons
from last year's growth,
they look with envy
at offspring of the tall ones
soon to be
oak, maple, poplar people.

True, they will die—
all beauty is terminal
when October's cold, hard nights fall,
but they come back—
their future ever brighter
as they climb toward the sun
while we are but one season

lamps with little oil

our only hope:
a photographer
or a woman
with pen and paper.

FEEDING THE FLOW

Farms are cathedrals
where primordial ritual and sacrament reign
though we lack written provenance.
Spring has many ceremonies and rites:
In late April we drag a table from the porch
out under the apple tree where
an offering is made
of winter's dried-up honey jars
for bees both wild and domestic
descending on white blooms.
Spring sun warms
the golden prize in the jars,
only a small golden ring
remaining at the bottom of each.
It seeps out onto a plate
where worker bees kneel at the amber alter
their humming liturgy sweet music to plant by.

Though it happens every time,
I stand always amazed.
The hidden bees appear
out of nowhere
summoned by something unseen—
a glyph in the clouds,
a whistle through the field of wild mustard
calling them to April vespers.
Forgotten in the winter ice and gray pelt sky,
taken for granted like mother's love,
they show up
whether we are grateful or not,
blindly assured
that the wild always comes through,
that Creation,
the Great Plan, will always work out,
whether we try or not.

Artfully arranging the row of jars
under the tree to take a picture,
I join the fight with sourness, too,
every way I can—
the bees and I carrying pollen and poems
unburdened by thought and fear
delivered from winter
and the grave and memory.
They are the honey from my days offered
to the ghostly gods,
legions of angels assigned
to keep check on the great flow,
that cosmic transparent eyeball keeping watch
on the seasons of it all.

Prayer of the Restless Son

Let me wake this day happy in my bed
tasting berries, cake and coffee
relaxed and rested
snatches of old tunes running in my head.

May I pay attention today
to the call of birds
first warm breath of spring
sunlight glinting off a pretty girl's long hair.

Help my daily disappointment
be brief as bubbles on Granddaddy's pond.
Lift me out of all yesterdays.
Plant my feet on the good road ahead.

Please grow me a new skin this day
new eyes, new hands, a new tongue
to drink up the new, spit out doubt
and name my future children
from the great beyond.

Mourning the Eclipse

Most days, clouds supply
the sun's scrim
but today
farmers' best friend and worst foe
will be conquered by the moon.

As always, I am prepared
perched on the farm's highest hill,
camera and extra lens
ready for the light to change,
welcoming epiphany through eclipse.

My husband has no time nor inclination
to seek out art.
Donning his broad-brimmed hat—
his own portable moon—
he begins his weekly mowing,
riding deep green sea
without even looking up
ribboning the lawn toward the tree line
where turkeys march,
where August thumps the ground
with perfect apples.
He smiles and waves
thinking of nothing but the work,
each swath he cuts under silvered sky
as satisfying as bread.

I smile back,
snap the photo of him
in mind's eye
without raising the camera.
I continue what I do best:
waiting and waiting,
the afternoon long and fruitless.

No opportunity today,
the light change barely noticeable.
Sun and moon don't align here.
Once again, the farm is not of the world.

Finally, I gather up and descend,
left with nothing for my trouble.
Oh well.
Let others wear paper glasses
so impressed by the infinite,
by the light coming and going,
yet they drive blind daily
ignoring the wondrous gloaming,
blind to bluebirds
sallying with barn swallows.
I live and walk in the poem
in the song
in the painting every day.

Work done, I join him
at the bottom of the hill
and we stroll together under the heat
of a billion rays sent out eons ago,
this farm our new creation—
Ruth and Boaz, sun and moon
heathen and believer,
the children—distant stars twinkling in the cold—
everything in orbit
around this mountain nebula,
its own flickering light and dark.

New Year's Resolution

The black pearl sea
laps at the wreckage I'm floating on where
people in beautiful clothes gather
to talk about how wonderful they all are, how
neat and good. In the dream their faces
are 3D vivid like a movie.
They look at me
out of the corner of their eyes
and lie and lie
while the willful wind
brushes my cheek
like a hand turning
my head toward the stars.

This year I pledge to take
more vitamin D to
prevent despair, depression, disgust
detachment, and most of all,
disappointment—the real cause
of death for almost every one of us
no matter what the doctor says.

This one is like a flipbook.
It just loops endlessly until
I wake and acquaintances
or people I'm not close to any more
are in mundane situations
speaking nonsense, Alice-in-Wonderland
jabberwocky over and over.
I rarely dream of my children,
my husband, parents,
brother, sisters—my subconscious mind
even has a subconscious mind
like a funhouse mirror.

This year I pledge to take
more vitamin L to replace
all I've lost.
I will forgive myself
for forgetting,
forgive myself for remembering,
no longer be the flat character
in someone else's story, will make
my heart murmurs speak up—
but most days I pledge
to just be still.
Be still.
Be. Still.

I lie down planning to dream
of trees I have loved—the one
with a swing, the one like Eve's, then
another one where the bees live,
where the crippled fox
sent me a poem across silent snow.
To go out on a limb means
you are going where it lives,
that fruit doesn't stand for anything else
only the way
forward to the next day.

Why I Write

I cannot draw, but write riddles here in this earth bowl we stew in. Saints and ancients
at safe distance, the canvas empty of all the messiness. The ribbon of trees,
Clinch Mountain's curves, all become symbol and portent. Flesh belongs
on the turkey in the oven, not this hot-sauced page. The white nothing
of the blank notebook—for philosophy, heaven, things dreamt,
imagined in pure form, clean and neat, not concrete, nothing
smart except the art of leaving everything out and lost.
How can we appreciate what we never seek?

A poem is a flute, not a shotgun. Let us play it, the song a riddle in tones. So what
if I've seen shooting stars, eclipses, ball lightning, dying foals, epic storms,
given all of them to the shotgun page, the colorless void, home
of the unborn? Let me write things without words—breathing,
blood moving through blue veins, the dumbstruck silence
of déjà vu, our first look at our mother's face, heartbreak
that leaves us dizzy, the long silence when we realize
here we're so completely and always
alone.

METAPHOR MOON

I hug myself under the cool eye
of the night sky
under an orb
surely emptied of meaning
by now after thousands of paeans
and scribbled drama,
each one dull as my housecoat:

> The moon is a silver teakettle
> pouring white tea.
> The moon is a silver pendant
> on black cloth chain over a mother's heart.
> The moon is a bowl of silver dust
> of burnt lists and letters.

Clouds roll over and once more
I am gilded, a fish girl
swimming in night air
soft as water.

> Hunter, Harvest, Corn
> Buck, Blood, Worm
> and Cold, so cold—
> names given for all the moons
> men need and follow.

By morning the teakettle,
pendant, and bowl
will all be empty
starting to work toward rising again,
now as the women of the night:
Maiden, Mother, and Crone—
one Holy Trinity of the feminine—
slice, crescent or full face
visible, invisible, growing, shrinking

while the sun blares on
unseen by the human eye.

How soft this light—
God's gift wrapped in darkness,
whether it is love or grief
luring you out under the stars,
your eyes big moons themselves.

This old girl in the third phase—
the Holy Spirit Moon—
knows the moon is just a torch
lighting the path to the next blinding,
God up there pleased
with the cleverness of it all.

Writer's Block

I am not writing today—
yet an exquisite red fox
dug for mice in the sawdust.
Pear blossoms opened fat silk arms,
caught the moon's overflow
pouring itself out
silver tea into the ridge's cup.

I am not writing now—
while the world masquerades,
sings a spring serenade.
Wind whistles through
leaf litter ankle deep.
Trees wake and tremble with birded limbs,
leaf buds lifting like prayers.

I am not writing these days—
yet above me starlings ricochet
black boomerangs in cloud banks,
a squirrel prays for hours
atop a cedar fence post—
vicar of the vines—
and absolves me for it all.

I am not writing today.

Fallow Fields

And so it is this farm is a thousand days of questions like "What's a meadow for?"
and all the other hackneyed metaphors for all the stones that look like faces,
and the stones white as bones and the fields covered in small shards of slate
like broken hearts offering answers no one wants to hear.

And so it is that the starlings and the bluebirds don't speak,
have no use for one another and the waxy soul inside the bee tree
protects its heart from even hearing the hum
and the coyote pack howls to the heavens pointing toward the silence.

And so it is that the world wants dancing lines
that burn like an open Bic Butane singeing a gnarled palm,
just pure stimulation, nothing slight or light or delicate,
nothing that can be mistaken for old or patient, just blind rushing of syllables
from the world's skin, not a thought in its head.

And so it is I stand here dumb and useless in
trampled fronds of something green and meaningful,
unwilling to make sounds just for the sake of saying I did,
letting frogs chorus on, birds shout letters and notes to indifferent air.

And so it is that silence is my source and I am blind as bark,
and just as bound, to woody phylum root tangles, dirt webs of time and loss,
already in the past and future at once and you are wasting your time judging me,
already a dream or breeze or storm, just beyond your outstretched hand.

About the Author

Rita Quillen's novel *Wayland*, a sequel to *Hiding Ezra*, was published by Iris Press in fall 2019. Her full-length poetry collection, *The Mad Farmer's Wife*, was published in 2016 by Texas Review Press and was a finalist for the Weatherford Award in Appalachian Literature from Berea College. *Hiding Ezra*, released by Little Creek Books, was a finalist for the 2005 DANA Awards. One of six semi-finalists for the 2012-14 Poet Laureate of Virginia, she has received three Pushcart nominations and a Best of the Net nomination in 2012. Read more at www.ritasimsquillen.com.

CPSIA information can be obtained
at www.ICGtesting.com
Printed in the USA
LVHW020230150920
665926LV00001B/64